PENGUINS

by Jenny Markert

Published in the United States of America by The Child's World®
1980 Lookout Drive • Mankato, MN 56003-1705
800-599-READ • www.childsworld.com

PHOTO CREDITS

© David Tipling/Alamy: 24
© DLILLC/Corbis: cover, 1
© Doug Allan/naturepl.com: 25
© Flip Nicklin/Minden Pictures: 19
© Gerald L. Kooyman/Animals Animals–Earth Scenes: 11
© infocusphotos.com/Alamy: 26–27
© Ingo Arndt/Minden Pictures: 21
© iStockphoto.com: Justin Horrocks: 3, 31
© Joe McDonald/Animals Animals–Earth Scenes: 17
© Martha Holmes/npl/Minden Pictures: 14–15
© Mitsuaki Iwago/Minden Pictures: 29
© Pete Oxford/naturepl.com: 23
© Peter Steyn/ardea.com: 13
© Rinie Van Meurs/Foto Natura/Minden Pictures: 9
© Robert Fried/Alamy: 5
© Tim Davis/Corbis: 6–7

ACKNOWLEDGMENTS

The Child's World®: Mary Berendes, Publishing Director;
Katherine Stevenson, Editor; Pamela Mitsakos, Photo Researcher;
Judy Karren, Fact Checker

The Design Lab: Kathleen Petelinsek, Design; Kari Tobin, Page Production

LIBRARY OF CONGRESS CATALOGING-IN-PUBLICATION DATA

Markert, Jenny.
  Penguins / by Jenny Markert.
     p. cm. — (New naturebooks)
  Includes index.
  ISBN-13: 978-1-59296-850-3 (library bound : alk. paper)
  ISBN-10: 1-59296-850-3 (library bound : alk. paper)
  1. Penguins—Juvenile literature. I. Title. II. Series.
  QL696.S473M35 2007
  598.47—dc22   2007000310

Table of Contents

On the cover: Emperor penguins like this one are the largest type of penguin.

Meet the Penguin!

To stay warm, penguins in cold areas often huddle together—sometimes by the thousands.

Penguins make a wide range of sounds for communicating. They communicate with body movements, too.

Far away in a frozen land, snowy winds howl. Icebergs float quietly. Waves slosh on the freezing shore. Suddenly, an animal shoots out of the cold water and lands on the ice. It shakes the water off its plump body and waddles away on two legs. What could this strange animal be? It's a penguin!

This gentoo penguin lives on the Antarctic Peninsula. Gentoos are the fastest penguin swimmers. They can reach speeds of up to 22 miles (35 km) per hour.

What Are Penguins?

Many ocean animals have coloring similar to penguins'—dark on top and light underneath.

Penguins' bodies take in lots of salt from the seawater. They get rid of extra salt through their bills.

Penguins are birds, but they can't fly. Instead, they spend most of their lives in the ocean. Their smooth, sleek bodies are perfectly shaped for swimming. Their wings are powerful **flippers**.

Penguins have white bellies and dark backs. Their coloring protects them from enemies. When they are swimming, penguins are hard to see. From below, their light bellies blend in against the water's sunlit surface. From above, their dark backs blend in with the ocean below.

You can see this king penguin's flippers as it swims near the surface. Like all penguins, it keeps its feet pointed backward. This helps it move quickly through the water.

Are There Different Kinds of Penguins?

Emperor and king penguins both have golden-orange ear patches. King penguins have slimmer bodies, longer bills, and more orange on the upper part of their bodies.

Scientists group penguins into at least 17 different kinds, or **species**. The species vary in size. Emperor penguins are the biggest. They can reach nearly 4 feet (1 m) tall and weigh about 90 pounds (41 kg). Fairy penguins are only 16 inches (41 cm) tall and weigh about 2 pounds (1 kg).

Different penguin species have different markings. Adélie (uh-DAY-lee) penguins are plain black and white, with white eyelids and red bills. African penguins have some black and white striping. Other types have some colorful bills or feathers. Gentoo penguins have bright red-orange bills and white patches behind their eyes. Rockhoppers have bright red eyes, red bills, and yellow eyebrows that end in long feathers. Macaroni penguins have even longer yellow feathers on their heads.

Along with macaroni penguins, rockhopper penguins (like this one) are called "crested penguins." Rockhoppers got their name because they hop along the rocky shores near their homes.

Where Do Penguins Live?

Antarctica is covered with snow and ice all year long. Emperor penguins are the only animals that spend the winter on the open Antarctic ice.

Penguins use their black-and-white colors to help them warm up or cool off. To warm up, they turn so their dark feathers soak up the sun. To cool off, they turn the other way.

Penguins live only in the southern half of the world. Some live in areas with mild or even hot weather. But many live much farther south, in regions that are very cold. Some penguins even live on the thick ice around the continent of Antarctica. Since they can't fly, penguins would be easy meals for land-dwelling **predators**. Most penguins live on islands or coastlines where there are few such predators.

Some kinds of penguins spend three-fourths of their time in the water. In fact, some kinds are at sea for months at a time. They come on shore only to have babies or to shed their old feathers.

These emperor penguins are huddling together during a winter storm.

How Do Penguins Move?

Penguins have three clawed toes on each foot. Their toes help them grip ice and slippery rocks.

Penguins usually waddle slowly. But they can put their heads down and run if they need to!

When they are out of the water, penguins stand on their fat little legs. They look awkward when they walk. They waddle because their short legs are set so far back on their bodies. When they get tired of waddling, some penguins plop down on their bellies. If the ground is icy, the penguins go "tobogganing"—sliding along on their bellies. Sliding is much faster than walking!

Here you can see a group of emperor penguins waddling and "tobogganing" in Antarctica.

In the water, penguins are sleek and fast. They have powerful flippers instead of wings. As they move their flippers, they seem to fly through the water. Their feet have webs of skin between the toes. The penguins' webbed feet and tails help the birds steer as they swim.

Sometimes penguins leap in and out of the water as they swim. This is called *porpoising*, because porpoises swim like that, too. Some kinds of penguins swim that way often. Others do it only when they are in danger. Sometimes penguins do the same thing when they need to get out of the water quickly. They swim fast, then shoot right out of the water and onto ice or rocks.

Zoom! This emperor penguin is shooting out of the water and onto the ice.

Most of the penguins' foods are near the surface, so the birds don't have to dive very deep. Their dives are usually less than a minute long. Emperor penguins sometimes dive deeper. One emperor penguin dove 1,755 feet (535 m) deep!

15

How Do Penguins Stay Warm?

Adult penguins shed their feathers, or molt, once a year. New feathers replace old, worn feathers that are no longer waterproof.

Penguins that live in colder areas have longer feathers and thicker fat layers than those that live in warmer areas.

Penguins are perfectly made for living in the cold. They have a warm coat of feathers. The outer feathers are packed tightly together. They are covered with a special oil the penguin makes inside its body. Penguins **preen** their feathers by running their bills along them to clean them and spread the oil. The oiled feathers make the penguins waterproof and windproof.

Beneath these outer feathers, penguins have a layer of warm, fluffy feathers called **down**. Under their skin, they have a thick layer of fat. The fat keeps the penguins warm, too. But sometimes penguins get too hot. When this happens, they fluff up their feathers so the warm air can escape.

Here you can see the feathers on a king penguin's flipper.

What Do Penguins Eat?

Penguins don't eat while they are molting. They can't go in the water safely until they have their new, waterproof feathers.

Some male penguins don't eat while they are mating and waiting for their eggs to hatch. Male emperor penguins might go as long as four months without eating.

Penguins are predators that find all their food in the ocean. Their **prey** are mostly fish and some squid. Some penguins eat tiny animals called krill.

Penguins hunt mostly by sight. They see very well underwater. When they come to the sunlit surface, their eyes change shape to match the changing light. As penguins swim along, they chase their prey and snatch it in their bills. Then they swallow it whole. A penguin's tongue is covered with rough, backward-pointing spines. The spines help the penguin hold onto slippery foods while it swallows them.

18

These krill are feeding just under the ice in Antarctica.

Do Penguins Have Enemies?

In some places, animals that people brought from other lands have gotten loose and started eating penguins. These **feral** animals include cats, rats, and ferrets.

Penguins are protected by law to keep people from hunting them or collecting their eggs. In some places, people still collect the eggs illegally.

Krill and fish aren't the only things that swim in the ocean! Many deadly predators live there, too. Sharks, sea lions, and killer whales are ocean predators that like to eat penguins. But the penguin's worst ocean enemy is the leopard seal. Leopard seals swim fast and can catch any penguin that isn't careful. Some other animals also like to eat penguin eggs and young on land. They include snakes, lizards, foxes, and seabirds such as skuas.

People have been penguins' enemies, too. Years ago, they hunted countless penguins to use their skins and feathers for clothes. They turned the penguins' fat into oil. They ate penguin meat and eggs.

Leopard seals like this one have very sharp teeth. These seals are aggressive and like to be left alone. They would even attack photographers if they got too close!

What Are Baby Penguins Like?

Some rookeries have hundreds of thousands of birds.

Most penguins go back to the same rookeries every year to have their young.

A male emperor penguin might lose almost of half of his body fat while taking care of his egg.

When the time is right, penguins come onshore to nest. Different species have different ways and places for nesting. Many kinds gather at huge nesting areas called **rookeries**. Some rookeries are far out on the snowy ice. Others are on rocky cliffs. In the rookery, each female lays her eggs—in most cases, two. Some penguins lay their eggs in nests made of stones or grass.

Emperor and king penguins lay only one egg, and they don't build nests at all. Instead, they balance a single egg on their feet! A thick fold of featherless skin covers the egg and keeps it warm. The father emperor penguin keeps the egg warm for weeks while his mate goes to sea to feed. When the egg is close to hatching, she comes back and takes his place. Then he can finally eat!

These chinstrap penguins are nesting in a rookery on the South Sandwich Islands.

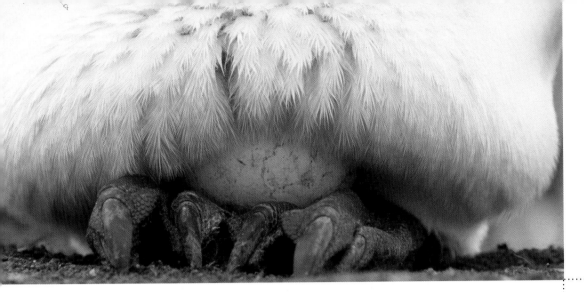

This king penguin is keeping its egg covered.

When the eggs are ready, the penguin chicks start to break out of their shells. They must do it without any help. They use a special *egg tooth* to chip and peck their way out. It can take up to three days for a chick to break out.

Penguin chicks don't look like their parents. They're covered with soft, fluffy down. The chicks often hide in their parents' feathers to keep warm. They eat food stored in their parents' throats. To find the food, the baby penguins stick their heads deep into their parents' mouths.

Chicks will try begging from any adult, but only their parents will feed them.

Some types of penguin chicks stay together in nursery groups while their parents look for food.

This emperor penguin chick looks very different from its parents. The photo on the cover of this book shows an adult emperor penguin.

25

In a huge rookery, penguins need a way to find each other and their chicks. They recognize each other by the sounds they make—even if there are thousands of birds!

The little penguins grow fast. They start to waddle around. Soon they lose their fluffy down and grow their next feathers. When the feathers are waterproof, the young penguins can start to go into the ocean. They take to swimming right away! Then they can start feeding themselves, too.

Rookeries are noisy places! But penguin chicks recognize their own parents' sounds right from the time they hatch.

These king penguins live in a huge rookery on South Georgia Island. The fluffy brown babies look much different from their parents! Even in such a large rookery, parents can find their own babies.

Are Penguins in Danger?

The population of New Zealand's yellow-eyed penguins has been dropping.

Penguins sometimes die from trash thrown in the ocean. They eat plastic or get tangled up in nets or lines.

Many penguins can live for 15 or 20 years in the wild. In zoos, they can live longer.

Some kinds of penguins are still doing well, but others are not. Some, such as the Galápagos penguin, are **endangered**. Like many other ocean animals, penguins face many dangers. They are easily harmed by oil spills and trash thrown in the ocean. They are also in danger if their ocean waters or land areas get warmer. And some kinds of penguins have lost their nesting areas as people have moved in. Luckily, people and governments around the world are working to protect these much-loved animals!

This Adélie penguin is right at home in the cold and snow!

Glossary

down (DOWN) Down is a layer of soft, fluffy feathers. Penguins' down helps keep them warm.

endangered (in-DAYN-jurd) An endangered animal is one that is close to dying out completely. Galápagos penguins are endangered.

feral (FER-ull) A feral animal is one that has gotten away from its owners and gone wild. Feral animals sometimes eat penguin eggs and young.

flippers (FLIH-purz) Flippers are broad, flat legs of some sea animals that act like paddles to help the animals swim. Penguins' wings have turned into flippers.

molt (MOLT) To molt is to get rid of an old outer layer of skin, shell, hair, or feathers. Penguins molt and grow new feathers every year.

predators (PREH-duh-terz) Predators are animals that hunt and kill other animals for food. Penguins are predators.

preen (PREEN) When birds preen their feathers, they slide their beaks along them to clean and tidy them. Preening helps penguins' feathers stay waterproof.

prey (PRAY) Prey are animals that other animals hunt as food. Penguins are prey for leopard seals.

rookeries (RUH-kuh-reez) Rookeries are large nesting areas used by many animals at once. Many penguins nest in rookeries.

species (SPEE-sheez) An animal species is a group of animals that share the same features and can have babies only with animals in the same group. There are at least 17 species of penguin.

To Find Out More

Watch It!

Jacquet, Luc. *March of the Penguins.* DVD. Burbank, CA: Warner Home Video, 2005.

Life in the Freezer. DVD. Burbank, CA: BBC Video, 2005.

The Penguins' Story. DVD. Escondido, CA: Tango Entertainment, 2006.

Read It!

Bredeson, Carmen. *Emperor Penguins Up Close.* Berkeley Heights, NJ: Enslow Elementary, 2006.

Gibbons, Gail. *Penguins!* New York: Holiday House, 1998.

Jacquet, Luc, Jordan Roberts, Jerome Maison, and Donnali Fifield. *March of the Penguins.* Washington, DC: National Geographic, 2006.

Kalman, Bobbie. *Penguins.* New York: Crabtree Publishing, 1995.

Lynch, Wanye. *Penguins!* Willowdale, Ont.: Firefly Books, 2001.

McGovern, Ann, and Colin Monteath. *Playing with Penguins and Other Adventures in Antarctica.* New York: Scholastic, 1994.

Stone, Lynn M. *Penguins.* Minneapolis, MN: Carolrhoda Books, 2003.

On the Web

Visit our Web page for lots of links about penguins:
http://www.childsworld.com/links

Note to Parents, Teachers, and Librarians: We routinely check our Web links to make sure they're safe, active sites—so encourage your readers to check them out!

Index

About the Author

Jenny Markert lives in Minneapolis, Minnesota, with her husband Mark and children, Hailey and Henry. She is a freelance writer and high-school American literature teacher who loves traveling and adventure in all forms, whether it's sailing the lake on a windy day, hiking the trails by moonlight, or helping her kids learn to boogie board when visiting the ocean. She is an animal lover and an environmentalist who believes, like the great American naturalist Henry David Thoreau, that "in wilderness is the preservation of the world." She is currently working on her second novel.